North Ayrshire Libraries

This book is to be returned on or before
the last date stamped below.

Most items can be renewed at
http://north-ayrshire.spydus.co.uk; download the
North Ayrshire Libraries App or by telephone.

My BIG ENGLISH-FRENCH Picture Dictionary

written by Catherine Bruzzone & Vicky Barker

illustrated by Vicky Barker

French adviser: Marie-Thérèse Bougard

www.bsmall.co.uk

Published by b small publishing ltd. www.bsmall.co.uk © b small publishing ltd. 2021 • 1 2 3 4 5 • ISBN 978-1-913918-30-9 •
Publisher: Sam Hutchinson   Art director: Vicky Barker   Editorial: Rachel Thorpe   Printed in China by WKT Co. Ltd.

Contents - Table des matières

tabl' deh mat-ee-err

hello
bonjour
bo(n)-shoor

Words and phrases - Les mots et les phrases
leh moh eh leh frahz

Essential words   Les mots essentiels

Word list   85-96   Vocabulaire

There are four words for 'the' in French:
le is for a masculine noun, singular
la is for a feminine noun, singular
l' is for a noun that starts with a vowel
or, in some cases, the letter h
les is for a plural noun

In French, nouns are either masculine
or feminine. The word for giraffe is feminine
(la girafe/les girafes) and the word for tiger
is masculine (le tigre/les tigres). This does not
mean that every giraffe is a girl and every tiger
is a boy! It does affect how you spell adjectives
describing them. See page 70.

At home - À la maison
ah la mezo(n)

door
la porte
la port

window
la fenêtre
la f'netr'

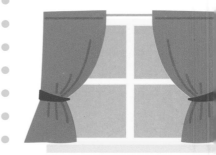

curtains
les rideaux
leh reed-o

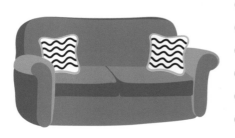

sofa
le canapé
ler kanap-eh

armchair
le fauteuil
ler foh-ter-yee

cushion
le coussin
ler kooss-a(n)

picture
le tableau
ler tablo

television
la télévision
la teh-leh-veezee-o(n)

phone
le téléphone
ler teh-leh-fon

Kitchen - La cuisine
la kweezeen

sink
l'évier
leh-vee-eh

fridge
le frigo
ler free-goh

hob
la plaque de cuisson
la plak der kweess-o(n)

oven
le four
ler foor

frying pan
la poêle
la poh-el

saucepan
la casserole
la kasserol

washing machine
le lave-linge
ler lav lansh

apron
le tablier
ler tab-lee-eh

kettle
la bouilloire
la boo-ywahr

Laying the table - Mettre la table

metr' la tabl'

knife
le couteau
ler kootoh

spoon
la cuillère
la kwee-yair

fork
la fourchette
la foor-shet

plate
l'assiette
lassee-et

glass
le verre
ler vair

teapot
la théière
la tayair

cup
la tasse
la tass

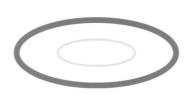

saucer
la soucoupe
la soo-koop

bowl
le bol
ler bol

Breakfast time - L'heure du petit-déjeuner

lerr doo p'tee desh-er-neh

table
la table
la tabl'

stool
le tabouret
ler taboo-reh

jug
le pichet
ler pee-sheh

cereal
les céréales
leh seh-reh-al

honey
le miel
ler mee-el

juice
le jus
ler shoo

jam
la confiture
la confeet-yoor

toast
le pain grillé
ler pa(n) gree-yeh

breakfast
le petit-déjeuner
ler p'tee desh-er-neh

Bedroom - La chambre
la shombr'

bed
le lit
ler lee

chest of drawers
la commode
la koh-mod

drawer
le tiroir
ler teer-wahr

wardrobe
l'armoire
larm-wahr

coat hanger
le cintre
ler santr'

alarm clock
le réveil
ler reh-vey

shelf
l'étagère
lehtah-shair

rug
le tapis
ler tapee

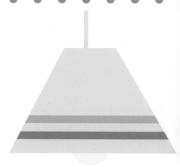

light
la lumière
la loom-ee-air

Goodnight, sweet dreams - Bonne nuit, fais de beaux rêves

bon nwee feh der boh rev

hook
le crochet
ler krosh-eh

teddy
le nounours
ler noo-noorss

bedside table
la table de nuit
la tabl' der nwee

lamp
la lampe
la lomp

blanket
la couverture
la koo-vairt-yoor

duvet
la couette
la koo-et

sheet
le drap
ler drah

pillow
l'oreiller
loray-eh

glasses
les lunettes
leh loon-et

9

Bathroom - La salle de bains
la sal-der-ba(n)

washbasin
le lavabo
ler lavaboh

toilet
les toilettes
leh twah-let

toilet paper
le papier-toilette
ler pap-ee-eh twah-let

shower
la douche
la doosh

bath
la baignoire
la bayn-wahr

tap
le robinet
ler rob-ee-neh

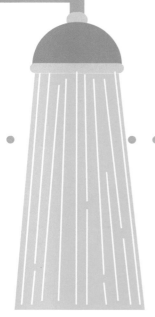

water
l'eau
loh

towel
la serviette
la sairvee-et

mirror
le miroir
ler meer-wahr

Wash your hands! - Lave-toi les mains !

lav twah leh ma(n)

toothpaste
le dentifrice
ler dontee-freess

toothbrush
la brosse à dents
la bross ah do(n)

soap
le savon
ler savo(n)

sponge
l'éponge
lep-onsh

bubbles
les bulles
leh bool

rubber duck
le canard en plastique
ler kanar o(n) plasteek

shampoo
le shampooing
ler shom-pwa(n)

hairbrush
la brosse à cheveux
la bross ah sher-ver

comb
le peigne
ler peh-ny'

11

Clothes - Les vêtements

leh vetmo(n)

skirt
la jupe
la shoop

dress
la robe
la rob

cardigan
le cardigan
ler kardee-go(n)

trousers
le pantalon
ler ponta-lo(n)

shirt
la chemise
la shem-eez

tie
la cravate
la krav-at

coat
le manteau
ler monto

shoes
les chaussures
leh showss-yoor

socks
les chaussettes
leh show-set

What are you wearing today? - Tu portes quoi aujourd'hui ?

too port kwah oh-shoor-dwee

T-shirt
le tee-shirt
ler tee-shirt

shorts
le short
ler short

jumper
le pull
ler pull

cap
la casquette
la kasket

boots
les bottes
leh bot

trainers
les baskets
leh basket

sandals
les sandales
leh sondal

vest
le débardeur
ler deh-bar der

pyjamas
le pyjama
ler peeshah-mah

13

Head and body - La tête et le corps

la tet eh ler cor

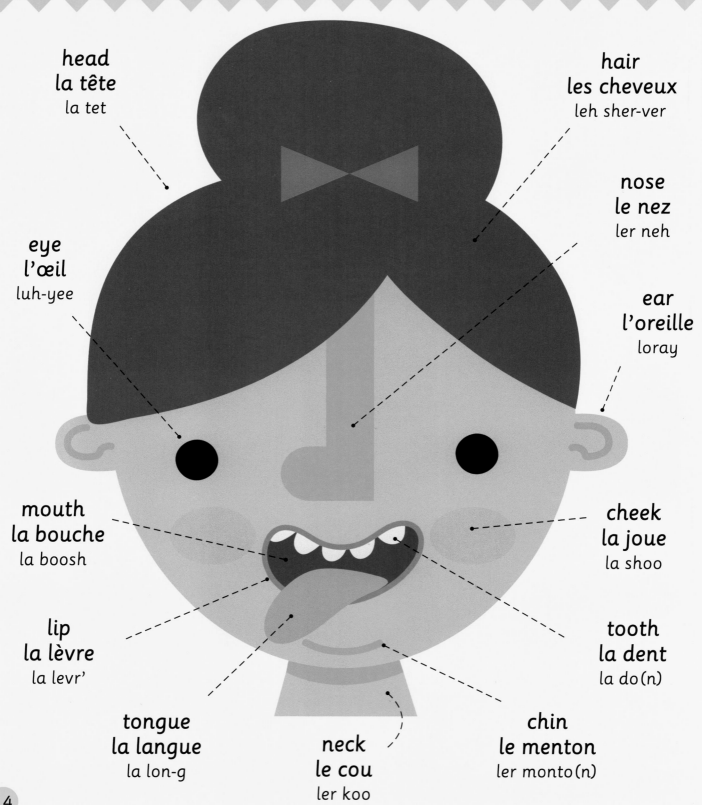

head
la tête
la tet

hair
les cheveux
leh sher-ver

eye
l'œil
luh-yee

nose
le nez
ler neh

ear
l'oreille
loray

mouth
la bouche
la boosh

cheek
la joue
la shoo

lip
la lèvre
la levr'

tooth
la dent
la do(n)

tongue
la langue
la lon-g

neck
le cou
ler koo

chin
le menton
ler monto(n)

Let's find ... - Trouvons ...
troo-vo(n)

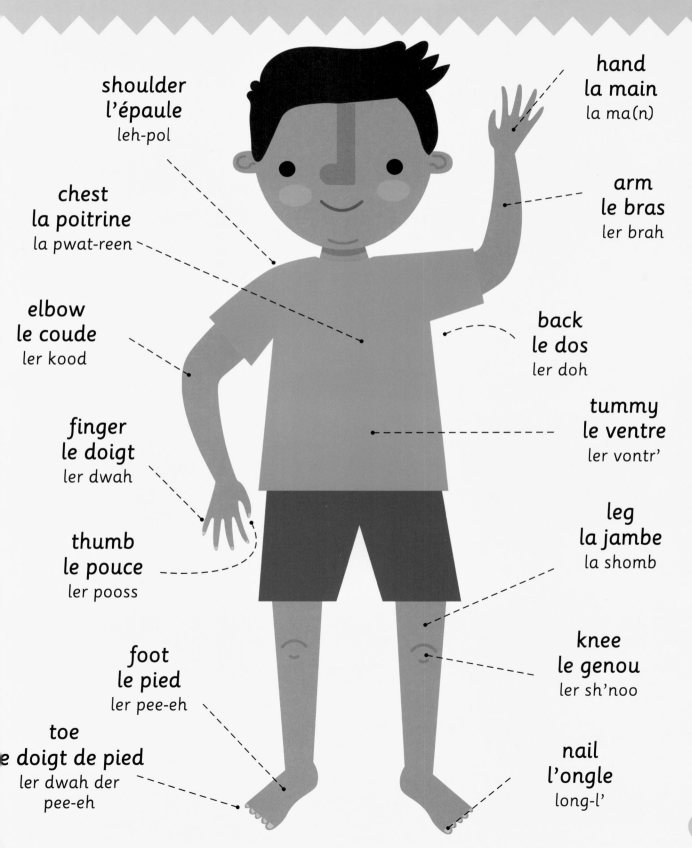

shoulder
l'épaule
leh-pol

chest
la poitrine
la pwat-reen

elbow
le coude
ler kood

finger
le doigt
ler dwah

thumb
le pouce
ler pooss

foot
le pied
ler pee-eh

toe
e doigt de pied
*ler dwah der
pee-eh*

hand
la main
la ma(n)

arm
le bras
ler brah

back
le dos
ler doh

tummy
le ventre
ler vontr'

leg
la jambe
la shomb

knee
le genou
ler sh'noo

nail
l'ongle
long-l'

15

Hospital - L'hôpital
lopeetal

doctor
le médecin
ler medsa(n)

doctor
la femme médecin
la fam medsa(n)

nurse
l'infirmier
lanfeerm-ee-eh

plaster cast
le plâtre
ler platr'

crutches
les béquilles
leh bek-ee

plaster
le pansement
ler po(n)-s'mo(n)

medicine
le médicament
ler medeeka-mo(n)

thermometer
le thermomètre
ler tair-moh-metr'

fever
la fièvre
la fee-evr'

Ouch! Does it hurt? - Aïe ! Ça fait mal ?
ay sa feh mal

nurse
l'infirmière
lanfeerm-ee-air

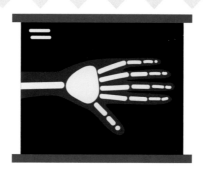

X-ray
la radio
la radee-o

bandage
le bandage
ler bon-daj-sh

tablets
les comprimés
leh kom-pree-meh

cough
la toux
la too

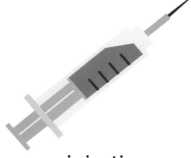

injection
la piqûre
la peek-yoor

headache
le mal de tête
ler mal der tet

tummy ache
le mal de ventre
ler mal der vontr'

blood
le sang
ler so(n)

Farm animals - Les animaux de la ferme

lez-anee-moh der la fairm

cow
la vache
la vash

calf
le veau
ler voh

mouse
la souris
la soo-ree

horse
le cheval
ler sh'val

foal
le poulain
ler pool-a(n)

donkey
l'âne
lahn

sheep
le mouton
ler moo-to(n)

lamb
l'agneau
lan-yoh

duck
le canard
ler kan-ar

Here are the baby animals - Voici les bébés animaux

vwa-see leh beh-beh anee-moh

cockerel
le coq
ler kok

hen
la poule
la pool

chick
le poussin
ler pooss-a(n)

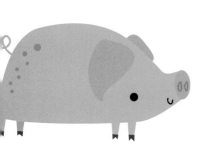

pig
le cochon
ler koh-sho(n)

piglet
le porcelet
ler por-ser-leh

goat
la chèvre
la shevr'

duckling
le caneton
ler kanet-o(n)

goose
l'oie
lwah

gosling
l'oison
lwah-zon

Wild animals - Les animaux sauvages

giraffe
la girafe
la shee-raf

hippopotamus
l'hippopotame
leepopotam

tiger
le tigre
ler teegr'

monkey
le singe
ler sansh

polar bear
l'ours blanc
loors blo(n)

lion
le lion
ler leeo(n)

elephant
l'éléphant
leleh-fo(n)

crocodile
le crocodile
ler krokodeel

gorilla
le gorille
ler gor-ee

kangaroo
le kangourou
ler kongoo-roo

brown bear
l'ours brun
loorss bran

koala
le koala
ler koala

rhinoceros
le rhinocéros
ler reenos-air-oss

panda
le panda
ler ponda

chameleon
le caméléon
ler kameh-leh-o(n)

zebra
le zèbre
ler zair-br'

bat
la chauve-souris
la showv-sooree

meerkat
le suricate
ler sooree-kat

Pets - Les animaux domestiques
lez anee-mo domesteek

cat
le chat
ler shah

kitten
le chaton
ler shat-o(n)

hamster
le hamster
ler amstair

dog
le chien
ler shee-ya(n)

puppy
le chiot
ler shee-oh

parrot
le perroquet
ler pair-o-keh

lizard
le lézard
ler lezar

snake
le serpent
ler sairpo(n)

guinea pig
le cochon d'Inde
ler kosho(n) dand

Birds - Les oiseaux

lez-wah-zo

ostrich
l'autruche
low-troosh

swan
le cygne
ler seen-yer

flamingo
le flamant
ler flam-o(n)

swallow
l'hirondelle
leeron-del

penguin
le pingouin
ler pang-wa(n)

owl
le hibou
ler eeboo

eagle
l'aigle
laygl'

pelican
le pélican
ler pel-ee-ko(n)

peacock
le paon
ler po(n)

23

Camping - Le camping
ler kompeeng

tent
la tente
la tont

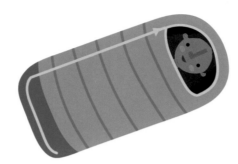

sleeping bag
le sac de couchage
ler sak der koosh-ajsh

camping chair
la chaise de campin
la shez der kompeeng

campfire
le feu de camp
ler fer der kom

mug
la tasse
la tass

map
la carte
la kart

compass
la boussole
la booss-ol

torch
la lampe torche
la lomp torsh

hammock
le hamac
ler amak

Flowers - Les fleurs
leh fler

daisy
la marguerite
la marg-er-reet

daffodil
la jonquille
la shonkee

rose
la rose
la roh-z

buttercup
le bouton d'or
ler boot-o(n) door

bluebell
la jacinthe des bois
la shasant deh bwah

lily
le lys
ler lees

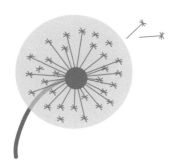

dandelion
le pissenlit
ler peess-o(n)-lee

snowdrop
la perce-neige
la pairs-nair'sh

tulip
la tulipe
la too-leep

25

Family - La famille
la famee

**grandfather
le grand-père**
ler gro(n)-pair

**grandmother
la grand-mère**
la gro(n)-mair

**mother/mummy
la mère/maman**
la mair/mamo(n)

**father/daddy
le père/papa**
ler pair/papa

**brother
le frère**
ler frair

**sister
la sœur**
la sir

Here is ... - Voici ...
vwahssee

aunt
la tante
la tohnt

uncle
l'oncle
lonkl'

nephew
le neveu
ler nev-e(r)

cousin
le cousin
ler kooza(n)

niece
la nièce
la nee-ess

cousin
la cousine
la koozeen

grandson
le petit-fils
ler p'tee-fees

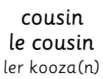

granddaughter
la petite-fille
la p'teet-fee

Playground - Le terrain de jeux
ler taira(n) der sher

swing
la balançoire
la balo(n)-swahr

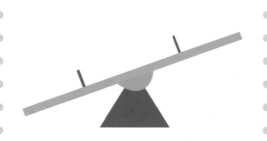

see-saw
la balançoire à bascule
la balon-swahr ah baskool

slide
le toboggan
ler tob-o-go(n)

sandpit
le bac à sable
ler bak ah sabl'

play area
l'aire de jeux
lair der sher

tunnel
le tunnel
ler too-nel

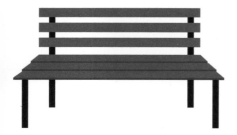

bench
le banc
ler bo(n)

path
le chemin
ler sher-ma(n)

picnic
le pique-nique
ler peek-neek

Park - Le parc

ler park

grass
l'herbe
lairb

pond
l'étang
leh-to(n)

stepping stones
les pierres de gué
leh pee-air der g-eh

tree
l'arbre
larbr'

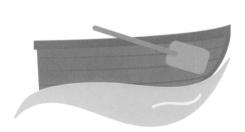

rowing boat
la barque
la bark

oar
la rame
la ram

bush
le buisson
ler bwee-so(n)

fountain
la fontaine
la fonten

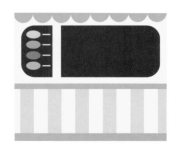

snack bar
le snack
ler snak

29

Toys - Les jouets

kite
le cerf-volant
ler sair-volo(n)

robot
le robot
ler roh-boh

ball
la balle
la bal

puzzle
le puzzle
ler puh-zl'

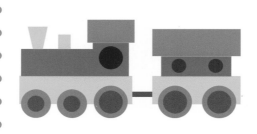

toy train
le petit train
ler p'tee tra(n)

doll
la poupée
la poo-peh

paints
les peintures
leh pant-yoor

paintbrush
le pinceau
ler pansso

magic set
l'ensemble de magi
lonsombl' der mashee

30

drum
le tambour
ler tomboor

costume
le costume
ler koss-toom

book
le livre
ler leevr'

puppet
la marionnette
la maree-on-et

guitar
la guitare
la g-eet-ar

skateboard
le skate
ler skate

xylophone
le xylophone
ler kseelo-fon

blocks
les cubes
leh kube

dinosaur
le dinosaure
ler deen-o-sor

Party - La fête
la fet

decorations
les décorations
leh deh-korass-eeo(n)

cake
le gâteau
ler gatoh

candle
la bougie
la boo-shee

ice-cream
la glace
la glass

sandwich
le sandwich
ler sondweech

chocolate
le chocolat
ler shokola

pizza
la pizza
la peet-sah

chips
les frites
leh freet

milkshake
le milkshake
ler meelk-shake

When is your birthday? - C'est quand ton anniversaire ?

seh ko(n) to(n) aneeversair

games
les jeux
leh sher

party dress
la robe de bal
la rob der bal

cupcakes
les cupcakes
leh kup-kek

balloon
le ballon
ler balo(n)

party hat
le chapeau pointu
ler shapo pwa(n)-too

music
la musique
la moo-zeek

magic wand
la baguette magique
la bag-et masheek

Happy birthday!
Joyeux anniversaire !
jwah-yerz anee-vairsair

present
le cadeau
ler kad-o

33

Telling stories - Raconter des histoires

rakont-eh dez-eestwaar

dragon
le dragon
ler drago(n)

mermaid
la sirène
la seeren

knight
le chevalier
ler sher-valee-yeh

fairy
la fée
la feh

witch
la sorcière
la sorsee-air

prince
le prince
ler pra(n)-ss

unicorn
la licorne
la leekorn

vampire
le vampire
ler vompeer

crown
la couronne
la koor-on

Let's play make-believe! - Jouons à faire semblant !

shoo-o(n) ah fer somblo(n)

sword
l'épée
leh-peh

helmet
le casque
ler cask

castle
le château
ler shato

princess
la princesse
la pra(n)-sess

king
le roi
ler rwah

queen
la reine
la ren

pirate
le pirate
ler peerat

pirate ship
le bateau pirate
ler bato peerat

treasure
le trésor
ler trezor

Transport - Le transport

bicycle
le vélo
ler veh-lo

motorbike
la moto
la moh-toh

scooter
le scooter
ler skoot-err

lorry
le camion
ler kamee-o(n)

van
la camionnette
la kameeo-net

pick-up truck
le pick-up
ler peek-up

scooter
la trottinette
la trot-een-et

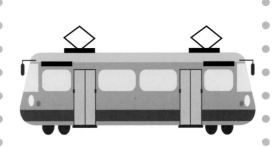

tram
le tram
ler tram

pushchair
la poussette
la pooss-et

Vroom, vroom! - Vroum, vroum !

vroom vroom

ambulance
l'ambulance
lamboolonss

fire engine
le camion de pompier
ler kamee-o(n) der pompee-eh

helicopter
l'hélicoptère
lelee-koptair

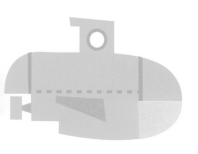

submarine
le sous-marin
ler soo-mara(n)

hot-air balloon
la montgolfière
la mongolf-ee-air

quad bike
le quad
ler qwad

cruise ship
le paquebot
ler pack-bo

tractor
le tracteur
ler trak-ter

taxi
le taxi
ler taxee

At sea - À la mer

ah la mair

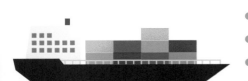

ship
le bateau
ler bato

oil tanker
le pétrolier
ler peh-trolee-yeh

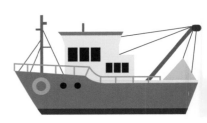

fishing boat
le bateau de pêche
ler bato der pesh

buoy
la bouée
la boo-eh

life belt
la bouée de sauvetage
la boo-eh der sowv-tah-jsh

lighthouse
le phare
ler far

anchor
l'ancre
lonkr'

life jacket
le gilet de sauvetage
ler shee-leh der sowv-tah-jsh

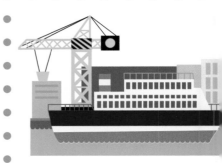

port
le port
ler por

38

Apartment building - L'immeuble
lee-mer-bl'

roof
le toit
ler twah

chimney
la cheminée
la sher-mee-neh

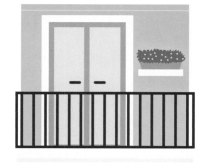

balcony
le balcon
ler bal-kon

flower pot
le pot de fleurs
ler po der fler

washing line
la corde à linge
la kord ah lansh

lift
l'ascenseur
lass-ons-err

garage
le garage
ler garah-jsh

recycling bin
le bac de recyclage
ler bak der reseek-lahjsh

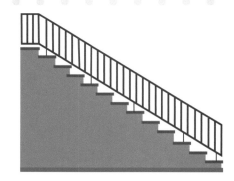

staircase
l'escalier
less-kalee-eh

Building site - Le chantier

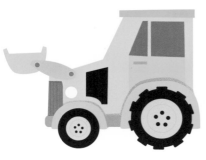

digger
la pelleteuse
la pelet-erz

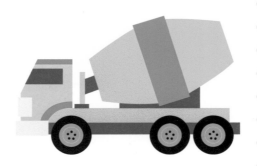

cement mixer
la bétonnière
la beton-yair

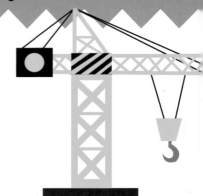

crane
la grue
la groo

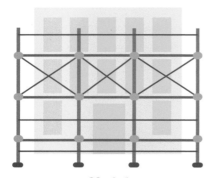

scaffolding
l'échafaudage
leh-shafo-dah-jsh

dumper truck
le camion benne
ler kamee-o(n) ben

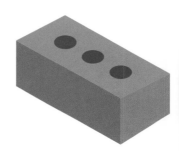

brick
la brique
la breek

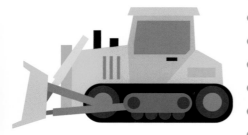

bulldozer
le bulldozer
ler bool-doh-zair

ladder
l'échelle
leh-shel

wood
le bois
ler bwah

Tools - Les outils
lez-oo-tee

rake
le râteau
ler rato

wheelbarrow
la brouette
la broo-et

hammer
le marteau
ler marto

nail
le clou
ler kloo

saw
la scie
la see

hose
le tuyau
ler twee-yoh

drill
la perceuse
la pair-serz

toolbox
la boîte à outils
la bwat ah oo-tee

screwdriver
le tournevis
ler toorn'veess

Travel - Le voyage
ler vwoyah-jsh

aeroplane
l'avion
lavee-o(n)

airport
l'aéroport
lah-airo-por

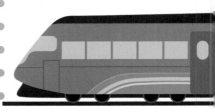

train
le train
ler tra(n)

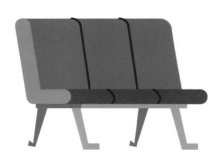

seat
le siège
ler see-esh

suitcase
la valise
la valeez

passport
le passeport
ler pass-por

purse
le porte-monnaie
ler port-moneh

trolley
le chariot
ler sharee-oh

seatbelt
la ceinture de sécurité
la sant-yoor der sek-yooree-teh

Let's go! - On y va !
o(n) ee va

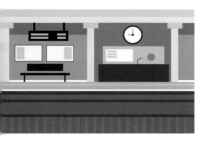

platform
le quai
ler keh

yacht
le yacht
ler yot

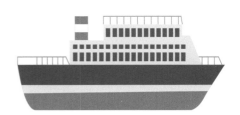

ferry
le ferry
ler fairee

ticket
le billet
ler bee-yeh

rucksack
le sac à dos
ler sak ah doh

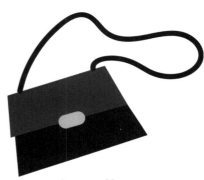

handbag
le sac à main
ler sak ah ma(n)

electric car
la voiture électrique
la vwat-yoor elek-treek

boot
le coffre
ler kofr'

driving
conduire
kondweer

43

In town - En ville
on veel

house
la maison
la mezo(n)

street
la rue
la roo

pavement
le trottoir
ler trot-wahr

street lamp
le lampadaire
ler lompadair

shop
le magasin
ler mag-ah-za(n)

bakery
la boulangerie
la boo-lonsh-airee

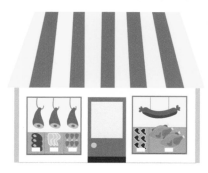

butcher
la boucherie
la booshair-ee

café
le café
ler cafeh

litter bin
la poubelle
la poo-bel

44

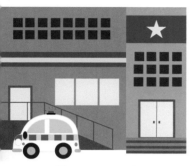

police station
commissariat de police
ler kom-eess-ariah deh poleess

police officer
le policier
ler poleess-ee-eh

police officer
la policière
la poleess-ee-air

post office
la poste
la post

postal worker
le facteur
ler fakt-err

postal worker
la factrice
la fakt-reess

postbox
la boîte à lettres
la bwat ah letr'

cinema
le cinéma
ler see-nay-mah

chemist
la pharmacie
la farmassee

45

Out on the road - Sur la route

car
la voiture
la vwat-yoor

traffic lights
les feux
leh fer

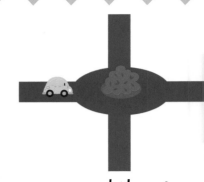

roundabout
le rond-point
ler ro(n)-pwa(n)

police car
la voiture de police
la vwat-yoor der poleess

school
l'école
leh-kol

factory
l'usine
loo-zeen

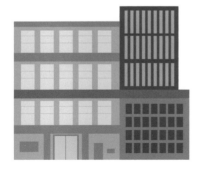

office
le bureau
ler byoo-ro

market
le marché
ler mar-sheh

hotel
l'hôtel
lotel

46

Where can you buy your lunch? - Tu peux acheter ton déjeuner où ?

too per ash'teh to(n) desh-er-neh oo

road
la route
la root

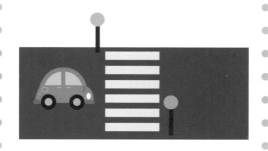

zebra crossing
le passage piéton
ler passah-sh pee-eh-to(n)

road sign
le panneau
ler pan-o

bus
l'autobus
low-toh-boos

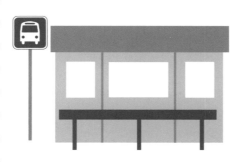

bus stop
l'arrêt d'autobus
larreh dow-toh-boos

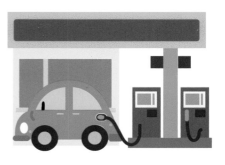

petrol station
la station-service
la stass-ee-o(n) serveess

supermarket
le supermarché
ler soo-pair-marsheh

car park
le parking
ler park-eeng

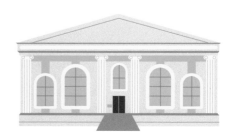

museum
le musée
ler moozeh

Supermarket - Le supermarché
ler soo-pair-marsheh

food
la nourriture
la nooreet-yoor

bread
le pain
ler pa(n)

meat
la viande
la vee-ond

rice
le riz
ler ree

fish
le poisson
ler pwah-sso(n)

butter
le beurre
ler ber

pasta
les pâtes
leh pat

sugar
le sucre
ler s'yoo-kr'

shopping trolley
le chariot
ler sharee-oh

What do you like to eat? - Tu aimes manger quoi ?

too em mansheh kwah

egg
l'œuf
lerf

cheese
le fromage
ler fromajsh

chicken
le poulet
ler poo-leh

sausage
la saucisse
la so-seess

milk
le lait
ler leh

yogurt
le yaourt
ler yah-oort

basket
le panier
ler panee-eh

shopping bag
le sac à provisions
ler sak ah proveez-yo(n)

money
l'argent
larsho(n)

Fruit - Les fruits
leh frwee

apple
la pomme
la pom

peach
la pêche
la pesh

cherries
les cerises
leh ser-reez

banana
la banane
la ban-an

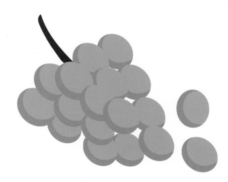

grapes
le raisin
ler reh-za(n)

strawberry
la fraise
la frez

watermelon
la pastèque
la pastek

melon
le melon
ler mer-lo(n)

coconut
la noix de coco
la nwah der koko

Which fruit is red? - Quel fruit est rouge ?

kel frwee eh roosh

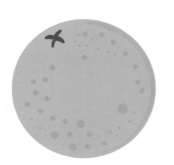

orange
l'orange
loronsh

pineapple
l'ananas
lan-ah-nass

mango
la mangue
la mong

lemon
le citron
ler seetro(n)

kiwi
le kiwi
ler kee-wee

pear
la poire
la pwahr

plum
la prune
la proon

blueberries
les myrtilles
leh meer-tee

raspberry
la framboise
la fromb-waz

51

Vegetables - Les légumes
leh leg-yoom

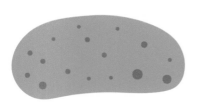

potato
la pomme de terre
la pom der tair

corn
le maïs
ler my-eess

cabbage
le chou
ler shoo

tomato
la tomate
la tom-at

lettuce
la laitue
la leh-too

cucumber
le concombre
ler ko(n)-kombr'

peas
les petits pois
leh p'tee pwah

pumpkin
la citrouille
la seetr-ee-yoo

broccoli
le brocoli
ler brok-o-lee

courgette
la courgette
la koor-shet

carrot
la carotte
la kah-rot

aubergine
l'aubergine
loh-bair-sheen

celery
le céleri
ler sel-air-ee

onion
l'oignon
lonyon

beans
les haricots
lez-aree-ko

avocado
l'avocat
lavo-ka

garlic
l'ail
la-yee

pepper
le poivron
ler pwah-vro(n)

53

Countryside - La campagne
la kom-pan-yer

woods
les bois
leh bwah

field
le champ
ler sho(n)

mountain
la montagne
la mon-tan-yer

windmill
le moulin à vent
ler moo-la(n) ah vo(n)

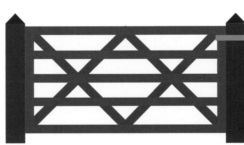

gate
le portail
ler porta-yee

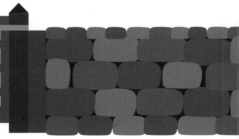

wall
le mur
ler myoor

badger
le blaireau
ler blair-o

fox
le renard
ler ren-ar

squirrel
l'écureuil
leh-kooray

54

Smell the fresh air! - Respire l'air frais !

respeer lair freh

stream
le ruisseau
ler rwee-so

waterfall
la cascade
la kaskad

bridge
le pont
ler po(n)

lake
le lac
ler lak

hill
la colline
la koleen

animal tracks
les empreintes
d'animaux
lez-omp-rant danee-moh

deer
le cerf
ler sair

rabbit
le lapin
ler lah-pa(n)

snail
l'escargot
less-kar-go

Forest - La forêt
la foreh

fir tree
le sapin
ler sapa(n)

trunk
le tronc
ler tro(n)

branch
la branche
la bronsh

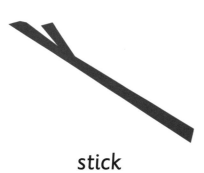

stick
le bâton
ler bato(n)

leaf
la feuille
la fuh-yee

pine cone
la pomme de pin
la pom der pa(n)

log
le rondin
ler ron-da(n)

petal
la pétale
la peh-tahl

root
la racine
la rah-seen

56

Insects - Les insectes
lez-ansekt

wasp
la guêpe
la g-ep

butterfly
le papillon
ler papee-o(n)

bee
l'abeille
la-bay

ladybird
la coccinelle
la coxee-nel

ant
la fourmi
la foor-mee

caterpillar
la chenille
la sher-nee

beetle
le scarabée
ler skah-rah-beh

fly
la mouche
la moosh

mosquito
le moustique
ler mooss-teek

57

Weather - Le temps
ler to(n)

sunshine
le soleil
ler solay

it is hot
il fait chaud
eel feh show

sunglasses
les lunettes de sole
leh loonett der solay

clouds
les nuages
leh noo-ajsh

wind
le vent
ler vo(n)

fog
le brouillard
ler brwee-ar

snow
la neige
la nair'sh

it is cold
il fait froid
eel feh frwah

gloves
les gants
leh go(n)

What a lovely day! - Quelle belle journée !

kel bel shoor-neh

rain
la pluie
la plwee

umbrella
le parapluie
ler pah-rah-plwee

puddle
la flaque d'eau
la flak doh

lightning
l'éclair
leh-klair

thunder
le tonnerre
ler tonair

storm
l'orage
lor-ah-jsh

ice
la glace
la glass

snowman
le bonhomme de neige
ler bonom der nair'sh

rainbow
l'arc-en-ciel
larkon-see-ell

Beach - La plage
la plaj-sh

sea
la mer
la mair

sand
le sable
ler sabl'

wave
la vague
la vag

seagull
la mouette
la moo-et

rock
le rocher
ler rosheh

seaweed
l'algue
lalg

shell
le coquillage
ler kokee-ajsh

deckchair
la chaise longue
la shez long

sun cream
la crème solaire
la krem solair

What can you see? - Tu vois quoi ?
too vwah koi

beach umbrella
le parasol
ler parasol

bucket
le seau
ler soh

spade
la pelle
la pel

sun hat
le chapeau de soleil
ler shapo der solay

rubber ring
la bouée
la boo-eh

sandcastle
le château de sable
ler shato der sabl'

surfboard
la planche de surf
la plo(n)-sh der serf

surfer
le surfeur/la surfeuse
ler serf-err/la serf-erz

sailing boat
le voilier
ler vwalee-eh

Under the sea - Le monde sous-marin

dolphin
le dauphin
ler doh-fa(n)

crab
le crabe
ler krab

turtle
la tortue
la tortoo

octopus
la pieuvre
la pee-er-vr'

shark
le requin
ler rek-a(n)

whale
la baleine
la balen

jellyfish
la méduse
la medooz

starfish
l'étoile de mer
leh-twal der mair

scuba diving
la plongée
la plonsheh

62

Earth
la Terre
la tair

sky
le ciel
ler see-el

Sun
le soleil
ler solay

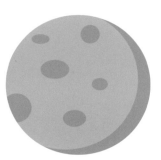

Moon
la lune
la loon

star
l'étoile
leh-twal

rocket
la fusée
la f'yoo-seh

planet
la planète
la plan-et

astronaut
l'astronaute
lastro-not

satellite
le satellite
ler satel-eet

At school - À l'école
ah lekol

teacher
le maître
ler metr'

teacher
la maîtresse
la met-ress

desk
le bureau
ler byoo-ro

pencil
le crayon
ler kray-o(n)

colouring pencils
les crayons de couleur
leh cray-o(n) der kool-err

chair
la chaise
la shez

glue
la colle
la koll

paper
le papier
ler pappee-eh

pen
le stylo
ler steelo

64

Back to school - La rentrée

rubber
la gomme
la gom

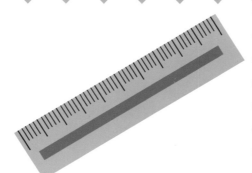

ruler
la règle
la regl'

scissors
les ciseaux
leh see-zoh

painting
le tableau
ler tablo

school bag
le sac à dos
ler sak ah doh

computer
l'ordinateur
lordeenat-err

bookshelf
la bibliothèque
la beebleeo-tek

exercise book
le cahier
ler kah-ee-yeh

clock
la pendule
la pond-yool

65

Sports - Le sport

football
le football
ler footbol

running
courir
kooreer

cycling
faire du vélo
fer doo vailo

skiing
faire du ski
fer doo skee

gymnastics
la gymnastique
la sheem-nass-teek

swimming
la natation
la natass-ee-yo(n)

athletics
l'athlétisme
lat-leh-tees-m'

tennis
le tennis
ler ten-eess

basketball
le basket
ler basket

I enjoy ... - J'aime ...
shem

horse riding
l'équitation
lehki-tass-eeo(n)

diving
plonger
plonsh-eh

climbing
grimper
gram-peh

walking
marcher
marsheh

sailing
faire de la voile
fer der la vwal

fishing
pêcher
pesheh

yoga
le yoga
ler yoga

doing a cartwheel
faire la roue
fair la roo

doing a handstand
faire l'arbre droit
fair larbr' drwah

Doing words - Les mots d'action
leh mo daksee-o(n)

crawling
ramper
rompeh

carrying
porter
porteh

kissing
embrasser
ombrass-eh

hugging
serrer dans ses bras
serreh do(n) seh brah

standing
être debout
etr' deboo

sitting
être assis/être assi
etr' assee/etr' asseez

pulling
tirer
teereh

pushing
pousser
poosseh

playing
jouer
shoo-eh

singing
chanter
shon-teh

reading
lire
leer

writing
écrire
eh-creer

drawing
dessiner
dess-een-eh

eating
manger
monsh-eh

drinking
boire
bwahr

washing
se laver
ser laveh

cleaning my teeth
se laver les dents
ser laveh leh do(n)

going to bed
aller au lit
al-eh o lee

Using adjectives - Les adjectifs
lez-adjekt-eef

Adjectives sometimes change depending on the gender of the noun that they are describing. Remember that the gender of a noun is not always related to the gender of the animal or person. The easiest rule to memorise is that adjectives describing feminine nouns usually have an 'e' on the end while those describing masculine nouns will not. The final part of a feminine adjective is pronounced with a stronger sound. See the examples below.

the elephant is big
l'éléphant est grand
leleh-fo(n) eh gro(n)

the whale is big
la baleine est grande
la balen eh grond

the rabbit is small
le lapin est petit
ler lah-pa(n) eh p'tee

the fly is small
la mouche est petite
la moosh eh p'teet

the boy is happy
le garçon est heureux
ler garso(n) eh err-er

the girl is happy
la fille est heureuse
la fee et err-erz

the boy is angry
le garçon est en colère
ler garso(n) eh o(n) kolair

the girl is angry
la fille est en colère
la fee et o(n) kolair

I am ... - Je suis ...
sh' swee

Some adjectives do not change at all, like '**sympa**' or '**triste**'. They are the same for both masculine and feminine nouns.

Words ending in '**x**' will add an '**se**'. This makes it easier to say, like '**heureuse**'.

kind
gentil/gentille
shontee/shontee

friendly
sympa
sampa

angry
en colère
on kolair

happy
heureux/heureuse
er-er/er-erz

sad
triste
treest

nervous
nerveux/nerveuse
ner-ver/ner-verz

brave
courageux/courageuse
koo-ra-sher/koo-ra-sherz

excited
enthousiaste
ontooz-ee-ast

71

Opposites - Les contraires
leh kontrair

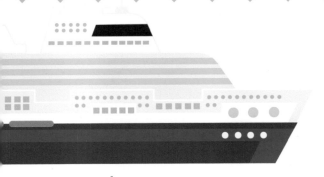

big
grand/grande
gron/grond

small
petit/petite
p'tee/p'teet

tall
grand/grande
gro(n)/grond

empty
vide
veed

full
plein/pleine
pla(n)/plehn

good
bon/bonne
bo(n)/bon

clean
propre
propr'

dirty
sale
sal

noisy
bruyant/bruyante
brwee-yo(n)/
brwee-yont

Who is ... ? - Qui est ... ?
ki eh

short
petit/petite
p'tee/p'teet

light
clair/claire
klair/klair

dark
foncé/foncée
fonseh/fonseh

bad
mauvais/mauvaise
moveh/movez

fast
rapide
rapeed

slow
lent/lente
lo(n)/lont

quiet
silencieux/silencieuse
see-lonsee-yer/
see-lonsee-yerz

strong
fort/forte
for/fort

weak
faible
febl'

73

on
sur
s'yoor

under
sous
soo

inside
à l'intérieur
ah lanteh-re-er

outside
dehors
der-or

in front of
devant
d'vo(n)

behind
derrière
dairee-air

up
en haut
o(n) oh

down
en bas
o(n) bah

near   **far**
près   **loin**
preh   lwah(n)

Questions! - Les questions !

leh kestee-o(n)

who?
qui ?
ki

what?
quoi ?
kwoi

when?
quand ?
ko(n)

where?
où ?
oo

why?
pourquoi ?
poor-koi

how?
comment ?
komo(n)

how much?
combien ?
kom-bee-a(n)

how many?
combien ?
kom-bee-a(n)

can I?
je peux ?
sh' per

Seasons and months - Les saisons et les mois

leh seh-zo(n) et leh mwah

spring
le printemps
ler pra(n)-tom

winter
l'hiver
lee-vair

summer
l'été
leh-teh

autumn
l'automne
lot-on

January
janvier
shon-vee-eh

February
février
feh-vree-eh

March
mars
marss

When is it hot? - Il fait chaud quand ?
eel feh show qo(n)

April
avril
av-reel

May
mai
meh

June
juin
shwa(n)

July
juillet
shwee-eh

August
août
oot

September
septembre
sep-tom-br'

October
octobre
ok-tobr'

November
novembre
no-vom-br'

December
décembre
deh-som-br'

Days of the week - Les jours de la semaine

leh shoor der la sermen

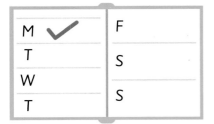

Monday
lundi
lern-dee

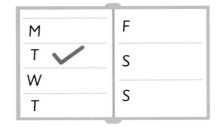

Tuesday
mardi
mar-dee

Wednesday
mercredi
mair-kr'-dee

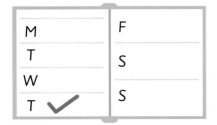

Thursday
jeudi
sher-dee

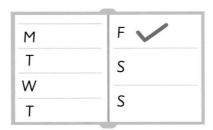

Friday
vendredi
vondr'-dee

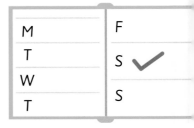

Saturday
samedi
samdee

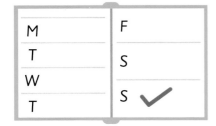

Sunday
dimanche
dee-monsh

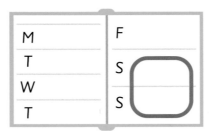

weekend
le week-end
ler week-end

On Mondays, I ...
Le lundi, je ...
ler lern-dee sh'

78

Useful words - Mots utiles
moh oo-teel

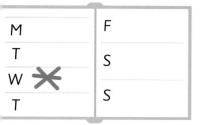

today
aujourd'hui
oh-shoor-dwee

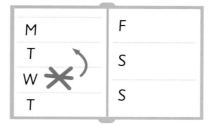

yesterday
hier
eeyair

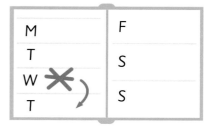

tomorrow
demain
der-ma(n)

morning
le matin
ler mat-a(n)

afternoon
l'après-midi
lap-preh mee-dee

evening
le soir
ler swahr

day
le jour
ler shoor

night
la nuit
la nwee

right
la droite
la drwat

left
la gauche
la goh-sh

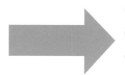

yes
oui
wee

no
non
no(n)

Colours - Les couleurs
leh kool-err

red
rouge
roosh

the coat is red
le manteau est rouge
ler monto eh roosh

the skirt is red
la jupe est rouge
la shoop eh roosh

blue
bleu/bleue
bl'/bl'

green
vert/verte
vair/vairt

yellow
jaune
shown

black
noir/noire
nwahr/nwahr

brown
marron
mah-ro(n)

white
blanc/blanche
blo(n)/blonsh

seh kwah ta koo-lerr pref-air-eh

orange
orange
oronsh

orange fox
le renard orange
ler ren-ar oronsh

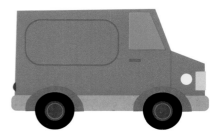

orange van
la camionnette orange
la kameeo-net oronsh

grey
gris/grise
gree/greez

pink
rose
roh-z

The word for the colour orange, '**orange**', is the same as the word for the fruit, 'l'**orange**'.

purple
violet/violette
veeoh-leh/veeoh-let

golden
doré/dorée
dor-eh/dor-eh

silver
argent
ar-sho(n)

81

Numbers - Les nombres

leh nombr'

1 one
un
ahn

2 two
deux
der

3 three
trois
trwah

4 four
quatre
katr'

9 nine
neuf
nerf

10 ten
dix
deess

11 eleven
onze
onz

15 *fifteen*
quinze
kanz

16 sixteen
seize
sez

17 *seventeen*
dix-sept
dees-set

Let's count together! - Comptons ensemble !

kon-to(n) onsombl'

5 *five*
cinq
sank

6 *six*
six
seess

7 *seven*
sept
set

8 *eight*
huit
weet

12 *twelve*
douze
dooz

13 *thirteen*
treize
trez

14 *fourteen*
quatorze
kat-orz

18 *eighteen*
dix-huit
dees-weet

19 *nineteen*
dix-neuf
dees-nerf

20 *twenty*
vingt
va(n)

High numbers - Les grands nombres

30
thirty
trente
tront

40
forty
quarante
karont

50
fifty
cinquante
sank-ont

60
sixty
soixante
swah-sont

70
seventy
soixante-dix
swah-sont-deess

80
eighty
quatre-vingts
katr'-va(n)

90
ninety
quatre-vingt-dix
katr'-va(n) dees

100
one hundred
cent
so(n)

1,000
one thousand
mille
meel

84

The most important words - Les mots les plus importants

leh moh leh ploos amport-o(n)

please
s'il te plaît
seel ter pleh

thank you
merci
mair-see

Word list - Vocabulaire

voh-kab-yoo-lair

Français/French – Anglais/English

l'abeille bee
l'aéroport airport
l'agneau lamb
l'aigle eagle
l'ail garlic
l'aire de jeux play area
l'algue seaweed
l'ambulance ambulance
l'ananas pineapple
l'ancre anchor
l'âne donkey
les animaux animals
les animaux domestiques pets
août August
l'après-midi afternoon
l'arbre tree
l'arc-en-ciel rainbow
argent silver
l'argent money
l'armoire wardrobe
l'arrêt d'autobus bus stop
l'ascenseur lift

l'assiette plate
l'astronaute astronaut (f/m)
l'athlétisme athletics
au revoir goodbye
l'aubergine aubergine
aujourd'hui today
l'autobus bus
l'automne autumn
l'autruche ostrich
l'avion aeroplane
l'avocat avocado
avril April
le bac à sable sandpit
le bac de recyclage recycling bin
la baguette magique magic wand
la baignoire bath
la balançoire swing
la balançoire à bascule see-saw
le balcon balcony
la baleine whale
la balle ball
le ballon balloon
la banane banana
le banc bench

le bandage bandage
la barque rowing boat
le basket basketball
les baskets trainers
le bateau ship
le bateau de pêche fishing boat
le bateau pirate pirate ship
le bâton stick
les béquilles crutches
la bétonnière cement mixer
le beurre butter
la bibliothèque bookshelf
le billet ticket
le blaireau badger
blanc/blanche white
bleu/bleue blue
boire drinking/to drink
le bois wood
les bois woods
la boîte à lettres postbox
la boîte à outils toolbox
le bol bowl
bon/bonne good
le bonhomme de neige snowman

bonjour hello
les bottes boots
la bouche mouth
la boucherie butcher (shop)
la bouée buoy
la bouée rubber ring
la bouée de sauvetage life belt
la bougie candle
la bouilloire kettle
la boulangerie bakery
la boussole compass
le bouton d'or buttercup
la branche branch
le bras arm
la brique brick
le brocoli broccoli
la brosse à cheveux hairbrush
la brosse à dents toothbrush
la brouette wheelbarrow
le brouillard fog
bruyant/bruyante noisy
le buisson bush
le bulldozer bulldozer
les bulles bubbles
le bureau desk
le bureau office
le cadeau present
le café café
le cahier exercise book
le caméléon chameleon
le camion lorry
le camion benne dumper truck
le camion de pompier fire engine
la camionnette van
la campagne countryside
le camping camping
le canapé sofa
le canard duck
le canard en plastique rubber duck
le caneton duckling
le cardigan cardigan
la carotte carrot
la carte map
la cascade waterfall
le casque helmet
la casquette cap

la casserole saucepan
la ceinture de sécurité seatbelt
le céleri celery
cent hundred
les céréales cereal
le cerf deer
le cerf-volant kite
les cerises cherries
la chaise chair
la chaise de camping camping chair
la chaise longue deckchair
la chambre bedroom
le champ field
chanter singing/to sing
le chantier building site
le chapeau de soleil sun hat
le chapeau pointu party hat
le chariot shopping trolley
le chariot trolley
le chat cat
le château castle
le château de sable sandcastle
le chaton kitten
les chaussettes socks
les chaussures shoes
la chauve-souris bat
le chemin path
la cheminée chimney
la chemise shirt
la chenille caterpillar
le cheval horse
le chevalier knight
les cheveux hair
la chèvre goat
le chien dog
le chiot puppy
le chocolat chocolate
le chou cabbage
le ciel sky
le cinéma cinema
cinq five
cinquante fifty
le cintre coat hanger
les ciseaux scissors
le citron lemon
la citrouille pumpkin

clair/claire light (colour)
le clou nail (tool)
la coccinelle ladybird
le cochon pig
le cochon d'Inde guinea pig
le coffre boot (of car)
la colle glue
la colline hill
comment how
le commissariat de police police
station
la commode chest of drawers
les comprimés tablets
le concombre cucumber
conduire driving/to drive
la confiture jam
les contraires opposites
le coq cockerel
le coquillage shell
la corde à linge washing line
le corps body
le costume costume
le cou neck
le coude elbow
la couette duvet
les couleurs colours
courageux/courageuse brave
la courgette courgette
courir running/to run
la couronne crown
court/courte short
le cousin cousin (m)
la cousine cousin (f)
le coussin cushion
le couteau knife
la couverture blanket
le crabe crab
la cravate tie
le crayon pencil
les crayons de couleur colouring
pencils
la crème solaire sun cream
le crochet hook
le crocodile crocodile
les cubes blocks
la cuillère spoon

la cuisine kitchen	**l'épaule** shoulder	**le frigo** fridge
les cupcakes cupcakes	**l'épée** sword	**les frites** chips
le cygne swan	**l'éponge** sponge	**le fromage** cheese
le dauphin dolphin	**l'équitation** horse riding	**les fruits** fruit
le débardeur vest	**l'escalier** staircase	**la fusée** rocket
décembre December	**l'escargot** snail	**les gants** gloves
les décorations decorations	**l'espace** space	**le garage** garage
dehors outside	**l'étagère** shelf	**le gâteau** cake
demain tomorrow	**l'étang** pond	**la gauche** left
la dent tooth	**l'été** summer	**le genou** knee
le dentifrice toothpaste	**l'étoile** star	**gentil/gentille** kind
derrière behind	**l'étoile de mer** starfish	**le gilet de sauvetage** life jacket
dessiner drawing/to draw	**être assis/être assise** to be sitting	**la girafe** giraffe
deux two	**être debout** to be standing	**la glace** ice
devant in front of	**l'évier** sink	**la glace** ice-cream
dimanche Sunday	**le facteur** postal worker (m)	**la gomme** rubber
le dinosaure dinosaur	**la factrice** postal worker (f)	**le gorille** gorilla
dix ten	**faible** weak	**la grand-mère** grandmother
dix-huit eighteen	**faire de la voile** sailing/to sail	**le grand-père** grandfather
dix-neuf nineteen	**la famille** family	**grand/grande** big
dix-sept seventeen	**le fauteuil** armchair	**grand/grande** tall
le doigt finger	**la fée** fairy	**grimper** climbing/to climb
le doigt de pied toe	**la femme médecin** doctor (f)	**gris/grise** grey
doré/dorée golden	**la fenêtre** window	**la grue** crane
le dos back	**la ferme** farm	**la guêpe** wasp
la douche shower	**le ferry** ferry	**la guitare** guitar
douze twelve	**la fête** party	**la gymnastique** gymnastics
le dragon dragon	**le feu de camp** campfire	**le hamac** hammock
le drap sheet	**la feuille** leaf	**le hamster** hamster
la droite right	**les feux** traffic lights	**les haricots** beans
l'eau water	**février** February	**l'hélicoptère** helicopter
l'échafaudage scaffolding	**la fièvre** fever	**l'herbe** grass
l'échelle ladder	**le flamant** flamingo	**heureux/heureuse** happy
l'éclair lightning	**la flaque d'eau** puddle	**le hibou** owl
l'école school	**les fleurs** flowers	**hier** yesterday
écrire writing/to write	**foncé/foncée** dark	**l'hippopotame** hippopotamus
l'écureuil squirrel	**la fontaine** fountain	**l'hirondelle** swallow
l'éléphant elephant	**le football** football	**l'hiver** winter
embrasser kissing/to kiss	**la forêt** forest	**l'hôpital** hospital
les empreintes d'animaux animal tracks	**fort/forte** strong	**l'hôtel** hotel
en bas down	**le four** oven	**huit** eight
en colère angry	**la fourchette** fork	**l'immeuble** apartment building
en haut up	**la fourmi** ant	**l'infirmier** nurse (m)
l'ensemble de magie magic set	**la fraise** strawberry	**l'infirmière** nurse (f)
enthousiaste excited	**la framboise** raspberry	**les insectes** insects
	le frère brother	**à l'intérieur** inside

la jacinthe des bois bluebell
la jambe leg
janvier January
jaune yellow
jeudi Thursday
les jeux games
la jonquille daffodil
la joue cheek
jouer playing/to play
les jouets toys
le jour day
juillet July
juin June
la jupe skirt
le jus juice
le kangourou kangaroo
le kiwi kiwi
le koala koala
le lac lake
le lait milk
la laitue lettuce
le lampadaire street lamp
la lampe lamp
la lampe torche torch
la langue tongue
le lapin rabbit
le lavabo washbasin
le lave-linge washing machine
les légumes vegetables
lent/lente slow
la lèvre lip
le lézard lizard
la licorne unicorn
le lion lion
lire reading/to read
le lit bed
le livre book
loin far
la lumière light (electric)
lundi Monday
la lune Moon
les lunettes glasses
les lunettes de soleil sunglasses
le lys lily
le magasin shop
mai May

la main hand
le maïs corn
la maison house
le maître teacher (m)
la maîtresse teacher (f)
le mal de tête headache
le mal de ventre tummy ache
la maman mummy
manger eating/to eat
la mangue mango
le manteau coat
le marché market
marcher walking/to walk
mardi Tuesday
la marguerite daisy
la marionnette puppet
marron brown
mars March
le marteau hammer
le matin morning
mauvais/mauvaise bad
le médecin doctor (m)
le médicament medicine
la méduse jellyfish
le melon melon
le menton chin
la mer sea
merci thank you
mercredi Wednesday
la mère mother
le miel honey
le milkshake milkshake
mille thousand
le miroir mirror
les mois months
la montagne mountain
la montgolfière hot-air balloon
la moto motorbike
la mouche fly
la mouette seagull
le moulin à vent windmill
le moustique mosquito
le mouton sheep
le mur wall
le musée museum
la musique music

les myrtilles blueberries
la natation swimming
la neige snow
nerveux/nerveuse nervous
neuf nine
le neveu nephew
le nez nose
la nièce niece
noir/noire black
la noix de coco coconut
les nombres numbers
non no
le nounours teddy
la nourriture food
novembre November
les nuages clouds
la nuit night
octobre October
l'œil eye
l'œuf egg
l'oie goose
l'oignon onion
les oiseaux birds
l'oison gosling
l'oncle uncle
l'ongle nail (body)
onze eleven
l'orage storm
l'orange orange (fruit)
orange orange (colour)
l'ordinateur computer
l'oreille ear
l'oreiller pillow
où where
oui yes
l'ours blanc polar bear
l'ours brun brown bear
les outils tools
le pain bread
le pain grillé toast
le panda panda
le panier basket
le panneau road sign
le pansement plaster
le pantalon trousers
le paon peacock

le papa   daddy
le papier   paper
le papier-toilette   toilet paper
le papillon   butterfly
le paquebot   cruise ship
le parapluie   umbrella
le parasol   beach umbrella
le parc   park
le parking   car park
le passage piéton   zebra crossing
le passeport   passport
la pastèque   watermelon
les pâtes   pasta
la pêche   peach
pêcher   fishing/to fish
le peigne   comb
les peintures   paints
le pélican   pelican
la pelle   spade
la pelleteuse   digger
la pendule   clock
la perce-neige   snowdrop
la perceuse   drill
le père   father
le perroquet   parrot
la pétale   petal
petit/petite   small
le petit-déjeuner   breakfast
le petit-fils   grandson
la petite-fille   granddaughter
les petits pois   peas
le petit train   toy train
le phare   lighthouse
la pharmacie   chemist
le pichet   jug
le pick-up   pick-up truck
le pied   foot
les pierres de gué   stepping stones
la pieuvre   octopus
le pinceau   paintbrush
le pingouin   penguin
le pique-nique   picnic
la piqûre   injection
le pirate   pirate
le pissenlit   dandelion
la pizza   pizza

la plage   beach
la planche de surf   surfboard
la planète   planet
la plaque de cuisson   hob
le plâtre   plaster cast
plein/pleine   full
la plongée   scuba diving
plonger   diving/to dive
la pluie   rain
la poêle   frying pan
la poire   pear
le poisson   fish
la poitrine   chest
le poivron   pepper (vegetable)
le policier   police officer (m)
la policière   police officer (f)
la pomme   apple
la pomme de pin   pine cone
la pomme de terre   potato
le pont   bridge
le porcelet   piglet
le port   port
le portail   gate
la porte   door
le porte-monnaie   purse
porter   carrying/to carry
la poste   post office
le pot de fleurs   flower pot
la poubelle   litter bin
le pouce   thumb
le poulain   foal
la poule   hen
le poulet   chicken (to eat)
la poupée   doll
pourquoi   why
pousser   pushing/to push
la poussette   pushchair
le poussin   chick
près   near
le prince   prince
la princesse   princess
le printemps   spring
propre   clean
la prune   plum
le pull   jumper
le puzzle   puzzle

le pyjama   pyjamas
le quad   quad bike
le quai   platform
quand   when
quarante   forty
quatorze   fourteen
quatre   four
quatre-vingt-dix   ninety
quatre-vingts   eighty
les questions   question
qui   who
quinze   fifteen
quoi   what
la racine   root
la radio   X-ray
le raisin   grapes
la rame   oar
ramper   crawling/to crawl
rapide   fast
le râteau   rake
la règle   ruler
la reine   queen
le renard   fox
le requin   shark
le réveil   alarm clock
le rhinocéros   rhinoceros
les rideaux   curtains
le riz   rice
la robe   dress
la robe de bal   party dress
le robinet   tap
le robot   robot
le rocher   rock
le roi   king
le rond-point   roundabout
le rondin   log
la rose   rose
rose   pink
rouge   red
la route   road
la rue   street
le ruisseau   stream
s'il te plaît   please
le sable   sand
le sac à dos   rucksack
le sac à dos   school bag

le sac à main handbag
le sac à provisions shopping bag
le sac de couchage sleeping bag
les saisons seasons
la salle de bains bathroom
sale dirty
samedi Saturday
les sandales sandals
le sandwich sandwich
le sang blood
le sapin fir tree
le satellite satellite
la saucisse sausage
le savon soap
le scarabée beetle
la scie saw
le scooter scooter (moped)
se laver washing/to wash
le seau bucket
seize sixteen
sept seven
septembre September
le serpent snake
serrer dans ses bras hugging/to hug
la serviette towel
le shampooing shampoo
le short shorts
le siège seat
silencieux/silencieuse quiet
le singe monkey
la sirène mermaid
six six
le skate skateboard
le ski skiing
le snack snack bar
la sœur sister
le soir evening
soixante sixty
soixante-dix seventy
le soleil Sun
le soleil sunshine
la sorcière witch
la soucoupe saucer
la souris mouse
sous under
le sous-marin submarine

le sport sports
la station service petrol station
le stylo pen
le sucre sugar
le supermarché supermarket
sur on
le surfeur surfer (m)
la surfeuse surfer (f)
le suricate meerkat
sympa friendly
la table table
la table de nuit bedside table
le tableau painting
le tableau picture
le tablier apron
le tabouret stool
le tambour drum
la tante aunt
le tapis rug
la tasse cup
la tasse mug
le taxi taxi
le tee-shirt T-shirt
le téléphone phone
la télévision television
le temps weather
le tennis tennis
la tente tent
le terrain de jeux playground
la Terre Earth
la tête head
la théière teapot
le thermomètre thermometer
le tigre tiger
tirer pulling/to pull
le tiroir drawer
le toboggan slide
les toilettes toilet
le toit roof
la tomate tomato
le tonnerre thunder
la tortue turtle
le tournevis screwdriver
la toux cough
le tracteur tractor
le train train

le tram tram
le transport transport
treize thirteen
trente thirty
le trésor treasure
triste sad
trois three
le tronc trunk (tree)
la trottinette scooter (child's)
le trottoir pavement
la tulipe tulip
le tunnel tunnel
le tuyau hose
un one
l'usine factory
la vache cow
la vague wave
la valise suitcase
le vampire vampire
le veau calf
le vélo bicycle/cycling
vendredi Friday
le vent wind
le ventre tummy
le verre glass
vert/verte green
les vêtements clothes
la viande meat
vide empty
la ville town
vingt twenty
violet/violette purple
le voilier sailing boat
la voiture car
la voiture de police police car
la voiture électrique electric car
le voyage travel
le week-end weekend
le xylophone xylophone
le yacht yacht
le yaourt yogurt
le yoga yoga
le zèbre zebra

Anglais/English – Français/French

aeroplane l'avion
afternoon l'après-midi
airport l'aéroport
alarm clock le réveil
ambulance l'ambulance
anchor l'ancre
angry en colère
animal tracks les empreintes
  d'animaux
animals les animaux
ant la fourmi
apartment building l'immeuble
apple la pomme
April avril
apron le tablier
arm le bras
armchair le fauteuil
astronaut (f/m) l'astronaute
athletics l'athlétisme
aubergine l'aubergine
August août
aunt la tante
autumn l'automne
avocado l'avocat
back le dos
bad mauvais/mauvaise
badger le blaireau

bakery la boulangerie
balcony le balcon
ball la balle
balloon le ballon
banana la banane
bandage le bandage
basket le panier
basketball le basket
bat la chauve-souris
bath la baignoire
bathroom la salle de bains
beach la plage
beach umbrella le parasol
beans les haricots
bed le lit
bedroom la chambre
bedside table la table de nuit
bee l'abeille
beetle le scarabée
behind derrière
bench le banc
bicycle le vélo
big grand/grande
birds les oiseaux
black noir/noire
blanket la couverture
blocks les cubes
blood le sang
blue bleu/bleue
bluebell la jacinthe des bois
blueberries les myrtilles
body le corps
book le livre
bookshelf la bibliothèque
boot (of car) le coffre
boots les bottes
bowl le bol
branch la branche
brave courageux/courageuse
bread le pain
breakfast le petit-déjeuner
brick la brique
bridge le pont
broccoli le brocoli
brother le frère
brown marron

brown bear l'ours brun
bubbles les bulles
bucket le seau
building site le chantier
bulldozer le bulldozer
buoy la bouée
bus l'autobus
bus stop l'arrêt d'autobus
bush le buisson
butcher (shop) la boucherie
butter le beurre
buttercup le bouton d'or
butterfly le papillon
cabbage le chou
café le café
cake le gâteau
calf le veau
campfire le feu de camp
camping le camping
camping chair la chaise de camping
candle la bougie
cap la casquette
car la voiture
car park le parking
cardigan le cardigan
carrot la carotte
carrying/to carry porter
castle le château
cat le chat
caterpillar la chenille
celery le céleri
cement mixer la bétonnière
cereal les céréales
chair la chaise
chameleon le caméléon
cheek la joue
cheese le fromage
chemist la pharmacie
cherries les cerises
chest la poitrine
chest of drawers la commode
chick le poussin
chicken (to eat) le poulet
chimney la cheminée
chin le menton
chips les frites

chocolate le chocolat	**decorations** les décorations	**family** la famille
cinema le cinéma	**deer** le cerf	**far** loin
clean propre	**desk** le bureau	**farm** la ferme
climbing/to climb grimper	**digger** la pelleteuse	**fast** rapide
clock la pendule	**dinosaur** le dinosaure	**father** le père
clothes les vêtements	**dirty** sale	**February** février
clouds les nuages	**diving/to dive** plonger	**ferry** le ferry
coat le manteau	**doctor (f)** la femme médecin	**fever** la fièvre
coat hanger le cintre	**doctor (m)** le médecin	**field** le champ
cockerel le coq	**dog** le chien	**fifteen** quinze
coconut la noix de coco	**doll** la poupée	**fifty** cinquante
colouring pencils les crayons de	**dolphin** le dauphin	**finger** le doigt
couleur	**donkey** l'âne	**fir tree** le sapin
colours les couleurs	**door** la porte	**fire engine** le camion de pompier
comb le peigne	**down** en bas	**fish** le poisson
compass la boussole	**dragon** le dragon	**fishing/to fish** pêcher
computer l'ordinateur	**drawer** le tiroir	**fishing boat** le bateau de pêche
corn le maïs	**drawing/to draw** dessiner	**five** cinq
costume le costume	**dress** la robe	**flamingo** le flamant
cough la toux	**drill** la perceuse	**flower pot** le pot de fleurs
countryside la campagne	**drinking/to drink** boire	**flowers** les fleurs
courgette la courgette	**driving/to drive** conduire	**fly** la mouche
cousin (f) la cousine	**drum** le tambour	**foal** le poulain
cousin (m) le cousin	**duck** le canard	**fog** le brouillard
cow la vache	**duckling** le caneton	**food** la nourriture
crab le crabe	**dumper truck** le camion benne	**foot** le pied
crane la grue	**duvet** la couette	**football** le football
crawling/to crawl ramper	**eagle** l'aigle	**forest** la forêt
crocodile le crocodile	**ear** l'oreille	**fork** la fourchette
crown la couronne	**Earth** la Terre	**forty** quarante
cruise ship le paquebot	**eating/to eat** manger	**fountain** la fontaine
crutches les béquilles	**egg** l'œuf	**four** quatre
cucumber le concombre	**eight** huit	**fourteen** quatorze
cup la tasse	**eighteen** dix-huit	**fox** le renard
cupcakes les cupcakes	**eighty** quatre-vingts	**Friday** vendredi
curtains les rideaux	**elbow** le coude	**fridge** le frigo
cushion le coussin	**electric car** la voiture électrique	**friendly** sympa
cycling le vélo	**elephant** l'éléphant	**fruit** les fruits
daddy papa	**eleven** onze	**frying pan** la poêle
daffodil la jonquille	**empty** vide	**full** plein/pleine
daisy la marguerite	**evening** le soir	**games** les jeux
dandelion le pissenlit	**excited** enthousiaste	**garage** le garage
dark foncé/foncée	**exercise book** le cahier	**garlic** l'ail
day le jour	**eye** l'œil	**gate** le portail
December décembre	**factory** l'usine	**giraffe** la girafe
deckchair la chaise longue	**fairy** la fée	**glass** le verre

glasses   les lunettes
gloves   les gants
glue   la colle
goat   la chèvre
golden   doré/dorée
good   bon/bonne
goodbye   au revoir
goose   l'oie
gorilla   le gorille
gosling   l'oison
granddaughter   la petite-fille
grandfather   le grand-père
grandmother   la grand-mère
grandson   le petit-fils
grapes   le raisin
grass   l'herbe
green   vert/verte
grey   gris/grise
guinea pig   le cochon d'Inde
guitar   la guitare
gymnastics   la gymnastique
hair   les cheveux
hairbrush   la brosse à cheveux
hammer   le marteau
hammock   le hamac
hamster   le hamster
hand   la main
handbag   le sac à main
happy   heureux/heureuse
head   la tête
headache   le mal de tête
helicopter   l'hélicoptère
hello   bonjour
helmet   le casque
hen   la poule
hill   la colline
hippopotamus   l'hippopotame
hob   la plaque de cuisson
honey   le miel
hook   le crochet
horse   le cheval
horse riding   l'équitation
hose   le tuyau
hospital   l'hôpital
hot-air balloon   la montgolfière
hotel   l'hôtel

house   la maison
how   comment
hugging/to hug   serrer dans ses bras
hundred   cent
ice   la glace
ice-cream   la glace
in front of   devant
injection   la piqûre
insects   les insectes
inside   à l'intérieur
jam   la confiture
January   janvier
jellyfish   la méduse
jug   le pichet
juice   le jus
July   juillet
jumper   le pull
June   juin
kangaroo   le kangourou
kettle   la bouilloire
kind   gentil/gentille
king   le roi
kissing/to kiss   embrasser
kitchen   la cuisine
kite   le cerf-volant
kitten   le chaton
kiwi   le kiwi
knee   le genou
knife   le couteau
knight   le chevalier
koala   le koala
ladder   l'échelle
ladybird   la coccinelle
lake   le lac
lamb   l'agneau
lamp   la lampe
leaf   la feuille
left   la gauche
leg   la jambe
lemon   le citron
lettuce   la laitue
life belt   la bouée de sauvetage
life jacket   le gilet de sauvetage
lift   l'ascenseur
light (colour)   clair/claire
light (electric)   la lumière

lighthouse   le phare
lightning   l'éclair
lily   le lys
lion   le lion
lip   la lèvre
litter bin   la poubelle
lizard   le lézard
log   le rondin
lorry   le camion
magic set   l'ensemble de magie
magic wand   la baguette magique
mango   la mangue
map   la carte
March   mars
market   le marché
May   mai
meat   la viande
medicine   le médicament
meerkat   le suricate
melon   le melon
mermaid   la sirène
milk   le lait
milkshake   le milkshake
mirror   le miroir
Monday   lundi
money   l'argent
monkey   le singe
months   les mois
Moon   la lune
morning   le matin
mosquito   le moustique
mother   la mère
motorbike   la moto
mountain   la montagne
mouse   la souris
mouth   la bouche
mug   la tasse
mummy   maman
museum   le musée
music   la musique
nail (body)   l'ongle
nail (tool)   le clou
near   près
neck   le cou
nephew   le neveu
nervous   nerveux/nerveuse

niece   la nièce
night   la nuit
nine   neuf
nineteen   dix-neuf
ninety   quatre-vingt-dix
no   non
noisy   bruyant/bruyante
nose   le nez
November   novembre
numbers   les nombres
nurse (f)   l'infirmière
nurse (m)   l'infirmier
oar   la rame
October   octobre
octopus   la pieuvre
office   le bureau
oil tanker   le pétrolier
on   sur
one   un
onion   l'oignon
opposites   les contraires
orange (colour)   orange
orange (fruit)   l'orange
ostrich   l'autruche
outside   dehors
oven   le four
owl   le hibou
paintbrush   le pinceau
painting   le tableau
paints   les peintures
panda   le panda
paper   le papier
park   le parc
parrot   le perroquet
party   la fête
party dress   la robe de bal
party hat   le chapeau pointu
passport   le passeport
pasta   les pâtes
path   le chemin
pavement   le trottoir
peach   la pêche
peacock   le paon
pear   la poire
peas   les petits pois
pelican   le pélican

pen   le stylo
pencil   le crayon
penguin   le pingouin
pepper (vegetable)   le poivron
petal   la pétale
petrol station   la station service
pets   les animaux domestiques
phone   le téléphone
pick-up truck   le pick-up
picnic   le pique-nique
picture   le tableau
pig   le cochon
piglet   le porcelet
pillow   l'oreiller
pine cone   la pomme de pin
pineapple   l'ananas
pink   rose
pirate   le pirate
pirate ship   le bateau pirate
pizza   la pizza
planet   la planète
plaster   le pansement
plaster cast   le plâtre
plate   l'assiette
platform   le quai
play area   l'aire de jeux
playground   le terrain de jeux
playing/to play   jouer
please   s'il te plaît
plum   la prune
polar bear   l'ours blanc
police car   la voiture de police
police officer (f)   la policière
police officer (m)   le policier
police station   le commissariat de
   police
pond   l'étang
port   le port
post office   la poste
postal worker (f)   la factrice
postal worker (m)   le facteur
postbox   la boîte à lettres
potato   la pomme de terre
present   le cadeau
prince   le prince
princess   la princesse

puddle   la flaque d'eau
pulling/to pull   tirer
pumpkin   la citrouille
puppet   la marionnette
puppy   le chiot
purple   violet/violette
purse   le porte-monnaie
pushchair   la poussette
pushing/to push   pousser
puzzle   le puzzle
pyjamas   le pyjama
quad bike   le quad
queen   la reine
question   les questions
quiet   silencieux/silencieuse
rabbit   le lapin
rain   la pluie
rainbow   l'arc-en-ciel
rake   le râteau
raspberry   la framboise
reading/to read   lire
recycling bin   le bac de recyclage
red   rouge
rhinoceros   le rhinocéros
rice   le riz
right   la droite
road   la route
road sign   le panneau
robot   le robot
rock   le rocher
rocket   la fusée
roof   le toit
root   la racine
rose   la rose
roundabout   le rond-point
rowing boat   la barque
rubber   la gomme
rubber duck   le canard en plastique
rubber ring   la bouée
rucksack   le sac à dos
rug   le tapis
ruler   la règle
running/to run   courir
sad   triste
sailing/to sail   faire de la voile
sailing boat   le voilier

sand le sable
sandals les sandales
sandcastle le château de sable
sandpit le bac à sable
sandwich le sandwich
satellite le satellite
Saturday samedi
saucepan la casserole
saucer la soucoupe
sausage la saucisse
saw la scie
scaffolding l'échafaudage
school l'école
school bag le sac à dos
scissors les ciseaux
scooter (child's) la trottinette
scooter (moped) le scooter
screwdriver le tournevis
scuba diving la plongée
sea la mer
seagull la mouette
seasons les saisons
seat le siège
seatbelt la ceinture de sécurité
seaweed l'algue
see-saw la balançoire à bascule
September septembre
seven sept
seventeen dix-sept
seventy soixante-dix
shampoo le shampooing
shark le requin
sheep le mouton
sheet le drap
shelf l'étagère
shell le coquillage
ship le bateau
shirt la chemise
shoes les chaussures
shop le magasin
shopping bag le sac à provisions
shopping trolley le chariot
short court/courte
shorts le short
shoulder l'épaule
shower la douche

silver argent
singing/to sing chanter
sink l'évier
sister la sœur
(to be) sitting être assis/être assise
six six
sixteen seize
sixty soixante
skateboard le skate
skiing le ski
skirt la jupe
sky le ciel
sleeping bag le sac de couchage
slide le toboggan
slow lent/lente
small petit/petite
snack bar le snack
snail l'escargot
snake le serpent
snow la neige
snowdrop la perce-neige
snowman le bonhomme de neige
soap le savon
socks les chaussettes
sofa le canapé
space l'espace
spade la pelle
sponge l'éponge
spoon la cuillère
sports le sport
spring le printemps
squirrel l'écureuil
staircase l'escalier
(to be) standing être debout
star l'étoile
starfish l'étoile de mer
stepping stones les pierres de gué
stick le bâton
stool le tabouret
storm l'orage
strawberry la fraise
stream le ruisseau
street la rue
street lamp le lampadaire
strong fort/forte
submarine le sous-marin

sugar le sucre
suitcase la valise
summer l'été
sun le soleil
sun cream la crème solaire
sun hat le chapeau de soleil
Sunday dimanche
sunglasses les lunettes de soleil
sunshine le soleil
supermarket le supermarché
surfboard la planche de surf
surfer (f) la surfeuse
surfer (m) le surfeur
swallow l'hirondelle
swan le cygne
swimming la natation
swing la balançoire
sword l'épée
T-shirt le tee-shirt
table la table
tablets les comprimés
tall grand/grande
tap le robinet
taxi le taxi
teacher (f) la maîtresse
teacher (m) le maître
teapot la théière
teddy le nounours
television la télévision
ten dix
tennis le tennis
tent la tente
thank you merci
thermometer le thermomètre
thirteen treize
thirty trente
thousand mille
three trois
thumb le pouce
thunder le tonnerre
Thursday jeudi
ticket le billet
tie la cravate
tiger le tigre
toast le pain grillé
today aujourd'hui

toe   le doigt de pied
toilet   les toilettes
toilet paper   le papier-toilette
tomato   la tomate
tomorrow   demain
tongue   la langue
toolbox   la boîte à outils
tools   les outils
tooth   la dent
toothbrush   la brosse à dents
toothpaste   le dentifrice
torch   la lampe torche
towel   la serviette
town   la ville
toy train   le petit train
toys   les jouets
tractor   le tracteur
traffic lights   les feux
train   le train
trainers   les baskets
tram   le tram
transport   le transport
travel   le voyage
treasure   le trésor
tree   l'arbre
trolley   le chariot
trousers   le pantalon
trunk (tree)   le tronc
Tuesday   mardi
tulip   la tulipe
tummy   le ventre
tummy ache   le mal de ventre
tunnel   le tunnel
turtle   la tortue
twelve   douze
twenty   vingt
two   deux
umbrella   le parapluie
uncle   l'oncle
under   sous
unicorn   la licorne
up   en haut
vampire   le vampire
van   la camionnette
vegetables   les légumes
vest   le débardeur

walking/to walk   marcher
wall   le mur
wardrobe   l'armoire
washbasin   le lavabo
washing/to wash   se laver
washing line   la corde à linge
washing machine   le lave-linge
wasp   la guêpe
water   l'eau
waterfall   la cascade
watermelon   la pastèque
wave   la vague
weak   faible
weather   le temps
Wednesday   mercredi
weekend   le week-end
whale   la baleine
what   quoi
wheelbarrow   la brouette
when   quand
where   où
white   blanc/blanche
who   qui
why   pourquoi
wind   le vent
windmill   le moulin à vent
window   la fenêtre
winter   l'hiver
witch   la sorcière
wood   le bois
woods   les bois
writing/to write   écrire
X-ray   la radio
xylophone   le xylophone
yacht   le yacht
yellow   jaune
yes   oui
yesterday   hier
yoga   le yoga
yogurt   le yaourt
zebra   le zèbre
zebra crossing   le passage piéton

goodbye
au revoir
or'vwahr

Where will languages take you?

Our books are designed to take the fear out of having a go at a new language. It's important to practise and learn from your mistakes!

50 French Phrases
978-1-913918-01-9   £6.99

Tina, the detective
978-1-905-710-57-7   £6.99

Stretch your imagination

Spend more time together

Understand the world

Visit our languages hub for:
- support from a like-minded community
- exclusive offers, discounts and new products in our newsletter
- expert resources to help you take those first steps in your language learning journey

Mix & Match Flash Cards
978-1-911-509-99-8   £7.99